Random Acts

Poems by
Anthony Fonseca

Photography by
Melissa Goldsmith

Anthony Fonseca

Random Acts

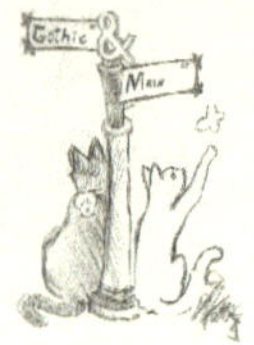

MLMC–Gothic and Main
Northampton, MA

Published by MLMC–Gothic and Main
29 Butler Place, #2
Northampton, MA 01060
http://www.mlmc-media.com

 Previous versions of some of these poems were published under the pseudonym M. A. Katz-Savoy in *Tri-Coastal and Other Poems.*

Cover photograph by Melissa Goldsmith
Gothic and Main logo by Renetta Hood.

ISBN 978-1-63328-009-0

TABLE OF CONTENTS

Morning Mirror 1

Certain Slant 2

Into the Dragon 3

The Other Side 5

Water Dance 6

Fly 7

Westside, San Antonio I 8

Saturday Prayer 10

City of Saints 11

Stasis 12

Westside, San Antonio II 14

Flag Day 15

Mia Tierra 16

Beach Buds 18

Valley Lightning 19

Snow Globe World 21

The Final Cut 23

Saturday Night, 1962 26

Death Bed 27

Random Acts Of 28

Alkylholics Anonymous 29

Amnesiac 31

Sampson My Brother 34

Sometimes 35

Cost of Living 37
For Willie 38
Wallace in Red Weather 39
Two Boys in Karbala 40
King Street 41
About the Author 42
About the Photographer 43

Morning Mirror

Creases
Drawn by dreams of the day before
Etched into this stranger's face
A reflection not quite recognizable
The name seems familiar,
The face escapes…
I have walked into the funhouse
Emotions stretched, disproportionate
Or multiplied infinitely, perhaps a smile
Knowing and mocking
Eyes retreating farther
Into the shadows
Not wanting to see
Into the abyss

Thoughts ride the creases like tracks
Through a private hall of mirrors
For now, they are free
Of the signs of moral decay
Safe from the impending
Collapse of time

Certain Slant

The sun's five fingers reach
through silver–lined clouds.
Transformed, the dark greens
of Texas hills and trees.
Brushstrokes that restore
the earth's distressed canvas.

They must have seen it.
Ancestors must have named it.
Miracle, God in the searchlights.
They must have thought
the outstretched hand
a personal greeting,
a friendly shoulder tap,
a gentle massage
after a long day.

I drive over one hill
towards another, indiscernible.
My windshield covered now—
Dust of the past,
remnants of memories,
long–gone friends.

The rays stretch out.

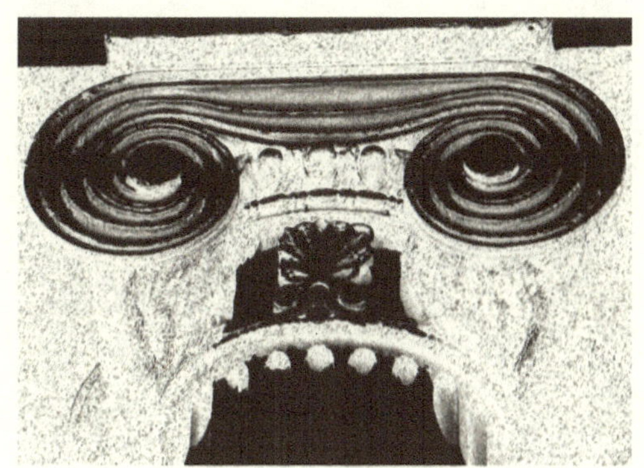

Into the Dragon

When I was a child
I used to think
the lights on the towers
windows
so round and so white
or stacks
of gold coins, a gilded city.

At day break, the stench
makes unmistakable
despite the fog
that slashes the tops
of buildings and towers
the oil refinery.

The Sunshine Bridge
stretches
across the Mississippi

It is a steel
dragon
straddling both banks
steam seeps from the
land itself
thick smoke that blinds.

We aim our headlights
at the lair's entrance,
accelerate
to ascension
our headlight beams
into the maw
of the metal beast.

Speeding towards the apex
the arched steel spine

Downward
We roll to the tail.
Where it guards
Towers of steam,
stacks
of gold.

And there
we slay or are slain.

The Other Side

the railroad divides worlds
St. Anthony's lost children:

a homeless beggar
scraggly beard
local radio–ad T–shirt

the words
"Fear This"

across his chest

crosses the tracks
joins others

huddled beside a brick shelter

under the overpass,

they sleep

without blankets,
without pillows,
without sheets

in fetal positions,
hands between legs
or
on their backs,
hands crossed serenely

ants crawl around and over them

nearby pigeons
fight for scraps

Water Dance

We were the only ones who saw it—
the end of May on Cape Cod,
still too cold for the bikini crowd,
and the wind blew fiercely,
holding the gulls in stasis—
just long enough for us to snap a photo.
Just you, and me, and the woman,
wearing her sweatshirt but still cold,
either oblivious or obstinate,
or like us, insistent. She sat on the rocks
alone, quiet, just staring into the Atlantic.
She did not know that we aimed our Nikon
at her, capturing the dance between her
wind-blown hair, the gray, crashing waves,
and the lone brave gull leaving its footprints in the sand.

Fly

A brown-skinned girl plays on her grandfather's farm,
chasing her brothers through gardens and ditches,
swerving down, curving back up. They run
to the back porch, proclaim it their "base,"
she turns and heads back, to dip, tumble, laugh.

Bright white teeth against his coal black face,
Grandfather watches from the kitchen window.
He knows his little miss does not have to think
of cotton, or whips, or backs red with blood,
of lost family, of being a commodity.

He watches and beams, he sees the young woman
who will not take flight when it's time to stand firm,
who will not weave in the face of fierce hatred,
who will not laugh when it's time to sit serious,
refusing to budge or leave when commanded.

He sees her at mid–age, eyes blazing, her lesson
that we own our minds, hearts, our mouths,
that we stand firm alone, firmer together,
that some are the head and some the back,
all are the mouth that speak community.

He sees her deathbed, her slight, serene smile,
as she dreams of that window, of his beaming face,
dreams of the girl, running, weaving, and laughing,
dreams of the horses, the carts, cars and planes,
of rockets soaring where she hopes to take wing.

Westside, San Antonio I

I.

Here the boys
in their ratty blue jeans
dirty red T–shirts
hold vases
with single red roses
both arms held high like
Mexico City athletes
with vase in each hand
signs that bark
FLOWERS FOR MOTHER'S DAY

II.

Packs of stray dogs
make their way around rusty pick–ups
old sky blue Oldsmobiles
bellow black smoke
here and there
brilliant reds, oranges, yellows
brighter than the morning sun
the family shops stand
gaudy and defiant

III.

I saw Frida
on the trolley today
smiling serenely

she stood in back
caressing an imaginary
metal guard rail

Diego in front, sitting,
talking with ghosts
rebellion, redemption

but not for her
doomed to vomit up
the eternal present

Saturday Prayer

Tonight let us don top hats,
tuxedo jackets made of black
cotton, plugs for our noses,
sun glasses in the dark, dressed
to the nines, our faces shine like
that of a refined corpse.

Let us lewdly dance and swear
in voices of thunder we will pray:
Lurer of the dead, lurid joker
of the cross and the criminal
loan to us this night, coarser minds—
Thoughts formed of smoke and rum.

Loaner of resurrections, Baron Sunday,
speak our names to Saint Vivienne
we who have to spirits gone, now found
at our crossroads, looking to be lead,
Jonesing to be saved by the magic black
caffeinated cure coursing our souls.

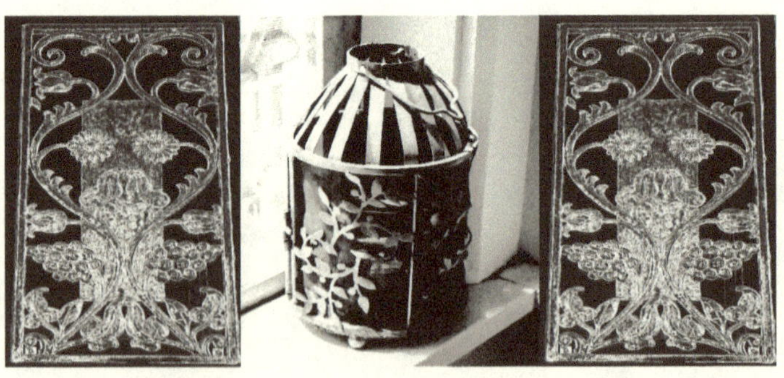

City of Saints

Drogo, patron saint of coffee shops
sips slowly on Sunday morning.
Francis smiles at every dog and owner.
Vivienne, head in hands, curses day—
After daylight. "She enjoys her Saturday
nights," jokes Mary Magdalen,
preening and brushing her hair.

People stop by the coffee house, sidle
up to the table, chat up the saintly crew:
How's tricks? Wuzzup? I need a favor. . . .
Unnerved but moved, they smile and nod.

Vitus does his best Brando, while George
tells jokes about driving out snakes.
"Are we there yet?"
And they all laugh, heavenly mirth,
hearing it the millionth time.

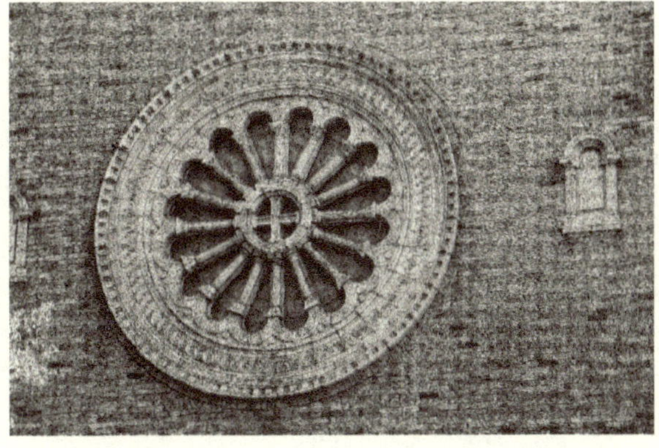

Stasis

Bayou trees stand
unmoved.
No wind looks
to brush their leaves.
Bark like marble,
leaves locked
in amber colored
still skies.

To say
the air stands still
is to look
at a snapshot.
For truth
is to listen
to cricket drone
for music.

H. D. saw heat,
but bayou sky has
weight.
A steel–toed work–boot
twisting downward.
This is the booted State.
Named after monarchy,
after oppression.

And the trees,
and the skies,
and the crickets
take no notice
of the unreal
stillness.

Westside, San Antonio II

I.

He walks by the shelter
His months old beard wire
His pink sweater too small
Minnie Mouse smiling
Hardly noticed by drivers

II.

A white woman weeps
Her head on the shoulder
Of a muscular black man
He holds her tightly
Neither aware of passing traffic
Or gray overcast skies

III.

Warrior camouflaged
In full fatigues
His heavy boots churn
Like the pistons of the passing
Cars he runs alongside
Gaudy painted rundown homes
His painted face expressionless
Running upright,
Holding high his American flag

Flag Day

The summer wind dies
Old Glory falls.
Limp, its contents,
melting, spilled whiteness.
Red waterfalls flow,
while below,
brown children
red to the knees. . . .

But one by one
they reach down,
pick up stars,
place them in pockets,
One by one.

Mia Tierra

It is like the skies burst open:
The raincloud a giant piñata
filled with colors unreal.
Then a crack of thunder
and Saint Anthony smiling,
wielding the winning bat

Colors rain down, surround you.
Some of them brighter than
sun rays, more striking than
lightning.

You cannot help but be struck.
The magic of divine preparation.
Everything becomes artifice—
Time ceases, life calcifies to art.

You cannot grow old.
And nothing can die
when the skies rain such colors.
Sweetness tempers ripeness.
Childhood tempers age.

Saintly artists paint the ceiling.
And you are tainted with beauty
and lost dreams of color, now found.

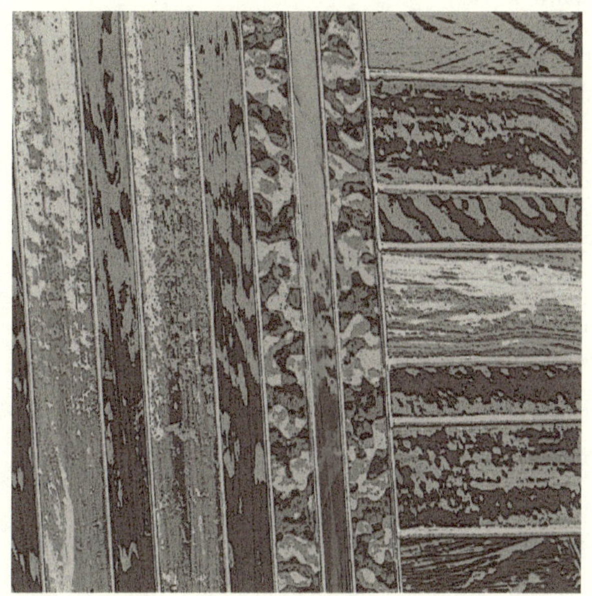

Beach Buds

The beach sand flows
Between my toes
Gulls hang in the sky
Whitewash approaches
Then it goes
Waving goodbye

We smile like the sun
As ocean foam rises
Crashes into the pier
Our lungs filled with
The breath of mist
The here and now

We huddle like gulls
Chasing crumbs on a beach
Our breath now filled
The mist of our smokes
That we pass along to friends
Silent as the sunset

Valley Lightning

The first thing that struck me was
the lack of rain, the dearth of the
deluge that you see along the Gulf
where rain is that insistent brother–in–law
who splashes into rooms like a belly–flopper,
demands attention's center of every parade.
Gulf Coast rain won't be ignored
It won't let up, it won't go away
and everything becomes rain
cars turn into pirogues,
shoes into boots,
land into swamp.

Nothing so mundane is the rain
that greets the valley, rather it
is the family manic–depressive, the sister,
or brother, or great–nephew who arrives
in a gray mist, a fog, an oppressive,
constant threat of cloudburst that waits
and waits, and waits, but instantly hits
with an impressive array of growls,
and groans, and streaks of moments so
electric as to make Armageddon into art
nothing changes once it passes
sunshine to sunshine,
dirt to dirt.

But you will remember that you were marked
at that moment, and knew myth, and power,
and what fear had to be, and you internalized
beyond the word, the essence of impressive.

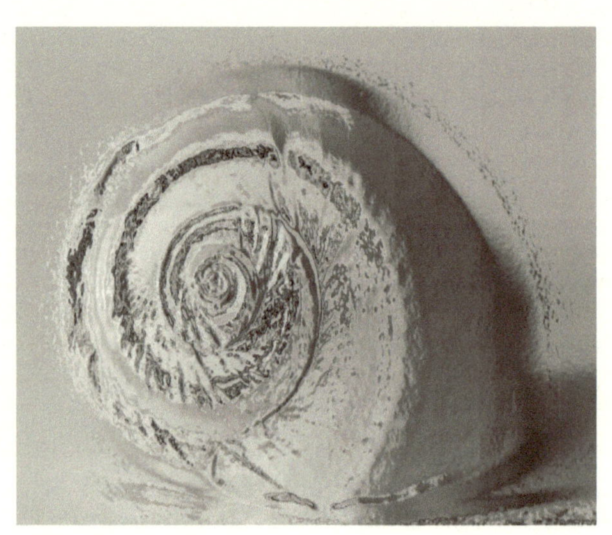

Snow Globe World

The ice couch on the screened in porch,
cars turned into mounds of snow,
iced branches and twigs, with no birds—
and icicles ten feet long hanging from
the neighbor's roof.

This snow globe world
of single–digit cold wants to freeze the spirit
and trap the body inside a heat filled house,
but there is something magical about the white
covered streets filled with child–like adults;
even the woman on cross–country snow skis
shows no sign of toil.

The world transformed—fun again:
just to walk through the icy pathways
reminds us that walking should be precarious,
an adventure waiting to unfold itself anew.

And every time we take the same well–worn path
layered up, we walk along and smile at each other
because we both have rediscovered something
once lost, or misplaced so deep inside that every
snowplow in the county would admit defeat
and head for the warmth of its garage home.
We pass the woman walking her prancing collie,
none of us feeling the bone–chill of the air.

It is winter, and soon we will wish for spring—
its colors a match for this beauty of solid white,
but for now, we wave and exchange smiles, and
hurriedly place our hands back in our pockets.

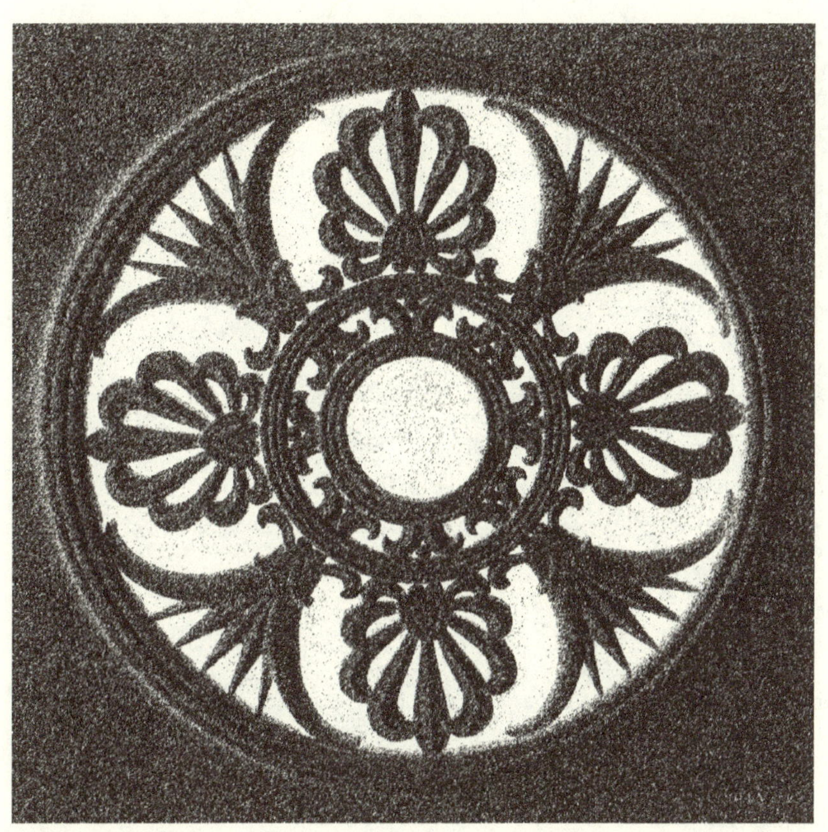

The Final Cut

When it was over, you held out the knife.
You were gloating,
the portrait of an artist of her own pain.

Your words, intended as blades,
their effect, more serrated
than sharp.

Then you showed me gifts,
self–inflicted items
bought to placate your
          self–hate.

But I thought,
better to spoil yourself
than cut yourself.

Too many days I relived
the first day
you told me,
"They held a knife to me.
One of them brought it down.
To my genitals. They
threatened to cut me.
I was so scared
being only twelve."

I was silent then.
But seeds were sown.

Tonight, when you held out your arm
I saw the new blossoms—
A garden of crimson twigs
over older weeds
going magenta to brown.

Deadhead them—
Their bloom will fade,
they will wither and fall:

Petal
by petal
by petal.

But you gather them up,
you press them to fill
the pages of memory.

Saturday Night, 1962

He stares at the fives, ones, quarters
enveloped by smoke, his eyes
slide back and forth, counting.
The four men bang cards at a table.
Domestic goddess on the silver screen,
Laura Petrie stands in her TV kitchen.

My mother sits and chuckles to herself.
Children gathered around. They half
listen to the men talk jobs and bosses.
She breathes easily, the haze unable
to choke her earned contentment.

My father questions his counts, curses
his luck, asks for coffee, spreads a new hand.
He concentrates harder.

She thinks
about cigarette butts, empty cups,
sticky beer cans and dirty glasses,
pots of beans, rices, breads, gumbos.
Then ironing shirts, folding towels, cleaning
rooms, about more children, more
mouths wrapped around needs and wants.

Laura stutters, "Oh Rob" on cue, and cans
of laughter erupt. The children cackle.
Silently, my mother goes to the cupboard.

Death Bed

"He could move like James Brown,"
my mother would say, recalling
the boy sliding across her floor.

I remember music.
He squats harmonica–happy,
a private tune to fill the void.
Skidrow the Scottie howling
in dog–harmony delight.

I still see him grinning,
rolling his smokes,
his private joke whizzing
over young heads that were unacquainted
with "Monsieur Zigzag."

And in smoke filled rooms,
the impossible shots he sank,
a cue stick geometry class of
lines, angles, backspin, speed.

We try to forget the dying man—
A skin–covered child skeleton,
eyes wide with cancer–fear,
veins pumping morphine,
12 minute intervals.

We stayed in turns, waiting.
We talked, eyes downcast, death
weighing every word,
each alone, we all jones
for the morphine of memory.

Random Acts Of

metallic ghosts
stand
in a fog of dust
debris
charred dreams
piles
where once stood
towers

divine
aspirations
concretized
not beautiful, but
wondrous
the human spirit
elevated

phantom like
white
muscle strained
humanity
tear–stained
eyes

visions of
glory
soot caked
tears
faces, lined with
defiance
they trudge
forward

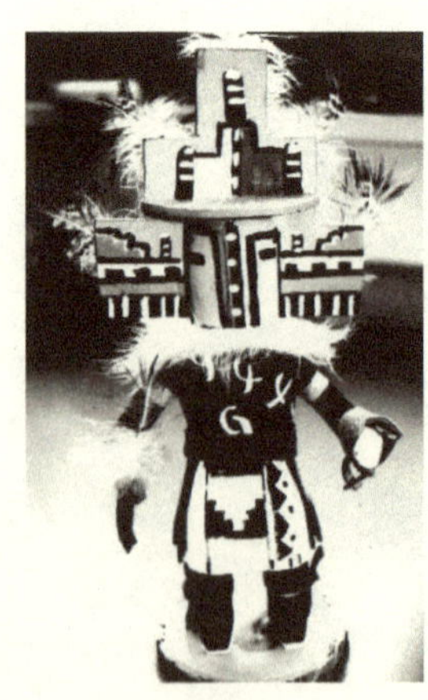

Alkylholics Anonymous

warm, dizzy, sense of
love
rather
relaxation
into the recreational
into the sexual
into the pleasurable

come to popper
is what he said
bring your hardware
he joked
get your 66 kicks and dis-
cover your quick-

Hi–Ho Silver

what a rush
like he was less un-
reactive, like he could be-
long to the func-
tional group
sudden
involuntary
just relax

is what his muscles said

flowers bloom from
glass seeds
yellow blossoms begging
to be inhaled
a cracking
a popping
a rebirth into

pleasure
a new you-

phoria
smoother
more in-
tense or-

chasm

eyes dilate blood flow heart free dilate sex as some-
thing
else
artifice
arteries

lapse momentary
recovery
to irony
a cure for his poisons
a cleaner for his viewing
pleasure

but to irony
his burned skin
his blurred vision

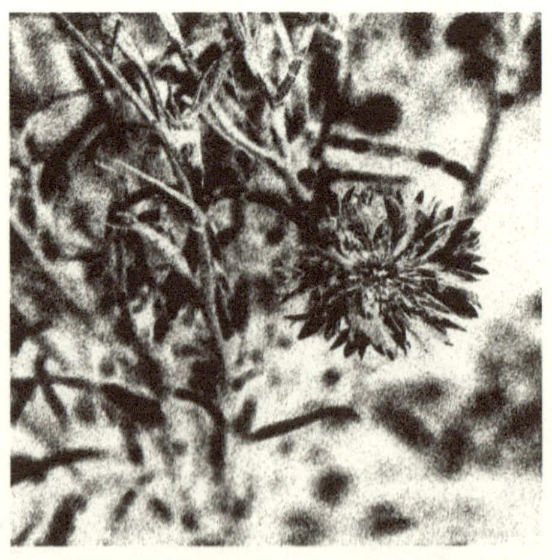

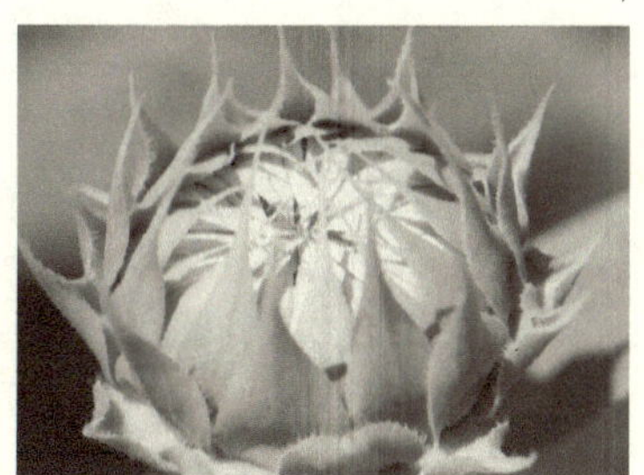

Amnesiac

I.

the first sound was inarticulate buzzing,
musical droning, oracular chanting of
a slow, steady melody, while gently
the keys to his emotions were fingered

he slowly opened his fists, digits spreading
to baby blue hues beyond his reaching,
the liquid world escaped his grasping,
pushed back, until ripples of white blinded

the first color was white, like
driving through fog, where
one can see, at best
ahead a few feet, yet

one always knows
the inevitability of destination

the second color was black
and it created life, outlines
and shadows:
buildings. trees. houses. people.

A cacophony of gray.

She laughs a hearty laugh
pours him a beer on tap
winks, and says, "man
is the animal that makes himself"
amused as she turns her back,
mumbles "trailing clouds of glory"

II.

he should have splashed like a raindrop
falling from the clouds, but balloon–like,
he got twisted into shapes by branches
barely discernable human form, folded
up on himself, he waited and rested,
nursing his bruises until ordered to move
a puppet with wrists and knees strung
his head was left hanging with each lift

he bobbed as he moved, lifting and falling
an awkward motion, his arms useless flapping
lifted up, dropped again, but always inching
forward, walking almost on his knees, scraping
the ground, sometimes his forehead touching,
stumbling ahead, he was lead to the

III.

Reflection:

sadness is a hue beyond blue
spirit darkening to purple shades
red thoughts ooze from the scalp
flowing downward to the chin
to meet lips, where words sit

Reflection:

IV.

black as charcoal on canvas
eyes gone from green to blue
to violet, but a sparkle, white
in each iris blends to become
yellow, broad brushstrokes
that are the shades of his face

Sampson My Brother

Dad used to yell at him, words
Pulling him back by his long hair
But he was quick out the door
Locks trailing in the wind
When he was a boy he once heard
That brushing hair makes it grow
So he grew his into a fortress
On which he could plant a flag
And he stood strong and proud
Until one day when cancer took his
Head into its lap, and ever so gently
Pulled at his hair until it all fell out

Sometimes

sometimes I stop
and watch closely
the tops of trees
as the breeze
passes gentle fingers
through the weakest limbs

sometimes while driving
through the fog
I am greeted by
disembodied smokestacks
bellowing steam
above the clouds

sometimes I imagine a line
like a steel wire
connecting the rose
to the farthest star
I engage with care
lest I float into space

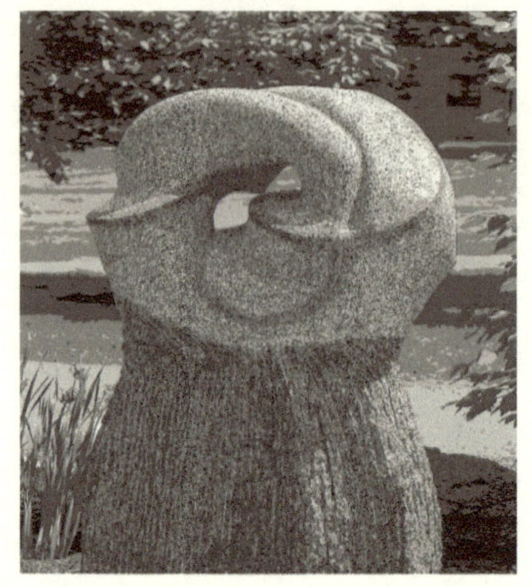

Cost of Living

Molested, impregnated,
giving birth at fifteen,
a mother thrice over.
switching men, like jobs
for the hopeless, the dreamless
the dark–skinned.

A life bought on minimum wage,
a stone heart and a love
of the grave at thirty.
her twelve grand a year,
the real wage of sin,
the price of a soul.

For Willie

he hears the crack
of wood on leather
up it soars
instinct tells him
run to the right
run to the wall
legs like pistons
leather whips out
to capture
the moment

Wallace in Red Weather

Words once haunted
by white and green,
stones on gold rings,
yellow sun dresses,
blue–blood speech
the power
of rhinestones.

Now he sings with
periwinkle
guitars,
thoughts drifts like a sailor
and sleep under stars.

Two Boys in Karbala

When he was twelve years old,
he did his father's bidding,
afraid of the old man's anger.
After all, they were invaders.
They would take his world by force.
They would kill his neighbors.
The other boy, twenty–one,
his uncle handed him total discretion
in life and death decisions, and
afraid of the ambush,
afraid of the young boy's rummaging,
he simply acted, pulled the trigger.

King Street

If you're going to walk
Down king street
Your eyes must be open
You head held high
Beware the sidewalks
They are paved with pitfalls
Fumes of oppression
Will fill the skies

If you're going to own
Your own journey
Be aware of the place
Where you stand
Cluttered paths will clear
As by magic if
You remember some
Slight of hand

Once you've crossed it
The sacred pathway
Once you've reached there
The other side
Roars of lizards
Long gone ages
Fade to silence
As you go by

The path's end
Is your destination, but
Your eyes must be open
You must hold your head high
Journey's end is but a list
Of overwhelming questions
The only answer
The big why

About the Author

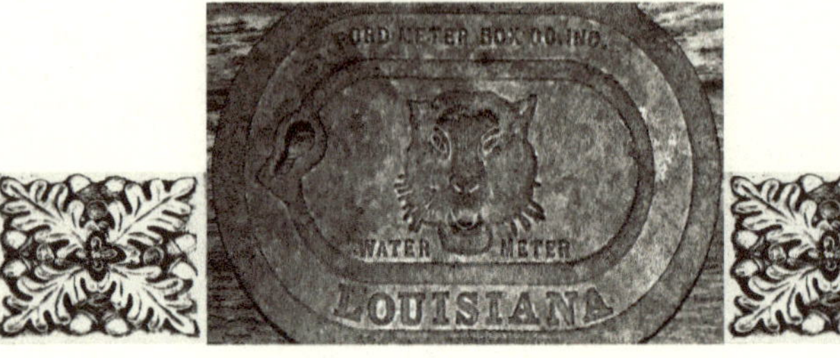

Anthony (Tony) Fonseca is a librarian living in Western Massachusetts. A native of Louisiana, he has lived in the South most of his life, but has become quite fond of actual seasons, multi-colored tulips, and sub-freezing, brisk days, quickly becoming a New Englander in spirit. He normally writes books on ghosts, vampires, zombies, and *The Twilight Zone,* and is a scholar of music and literature, but recently he has decided to venture into poetry, fiction, and song writing. *Random Acts* is his first book of poetry.

About the Photographer

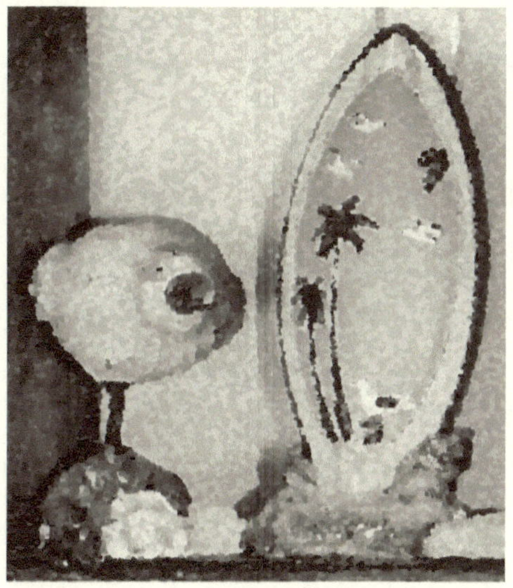

Melissa Goldsmith spent half of her childhood in Santa Monica and the other half in Santa Barbara. She is a professor of music who specializes in 20th-century music and aesthetics, and her passions include film music and rock and roll, as well as other forms of popular music. She has taught music, language, and writing courses in Louisiana and Massachusetts, where she currently resides. Her research, however, still takes her back to the West Coast and her childhood homes.

www.ingramcontent.com/pod-product-compliance
Lightning Source LLC
LaVergne TN
LVHW050947080826
845145LV00004B/1436

* 9 7 8 1 6 3 3 2 8 0 0 9 0 *